CW00402969

FRES
SUMMER
RECIPES WITH

FISH AND
SEAFOOD

Mirko Lotti

The benefits of summer seasonal food

You may have heard the term 'eat seasonally' touted by nutrition experts, foodies, and chefs alike. But what does that mean, and what are the benefits to eating seasonal foods? Also, what are the benefits of consuming foods from this season – summer! We'll discuss in this article.

Eating seasonally basically means including foods in your diet that are grown locally at the same time of year that you buy them. These days, due to importing/exporting practices and refrigerated transportation vehicles, we have an abundance of foods available from all over the world. This of course makes it easier to eat many foods, whether they are in season or not. However, there is more to eating seasonally than just a trendy term; there are many benefits to eating foods that are currently being grown and harvested.

How do you eat healthy?

People often think of healthy eating as dieting. This is not true. Eating healthy is not just about losing weight, it's about feeling better both physically and mentally. Eating healthy is about balance and making sure that your body is getting the necessary nutrients it needs to function properly. Healthy eating habits require that people eat fruits, vegetables, whole grains, fats, proteins, and starches. Keep in mind that healthy eating requires that you're mindful of what you eat and drink, but also how you prepare it. For best results, individuals should avoid fried or processed foods, as well as foods high in added sugars and salts.

The fundamentals of healthy eating

While some extreme diets may suggest otherwise, we all need a balance of protein, fat, carbohydrates, fiber, vitamins, and minerals in our diets to sustain a healthy body. You don't need to eliminate certain categories of food from your diet, but rather select the healthiest options from each category.

Top 5 Benefits of Healthy Eating

- Weight loss
- Heart Health
- Strong bones and teeth
- Better mood and energy levels
- Improved memory and brain health

Switching to a healthy diet doesn't have to be an all or nothing proposition. You don't have to be perfect, you don't have to completely eliminate foods you enjoy, and you don't have to change everything all at once—that usually only leads to cheating or giving up on your new eating plan.

To set yourself up for success, try to keep things simple. Eating a healthier diet doesn't have to be complicated.Focus on avoiding packaged and processed foods and opting for more fresh ingredients whenever possible.

- Prepare more of your own meals
- Make the right changes
- Read the labels
- Focus on how you feel after eating
- Drink plenty of water

Table of Contents

FROM THE SEA TO YOUR TABLE

Saffron Shrimp

Preparation time: 10 minutes

Cooking time: 30 minutes

Servings: 4

Ingredients:

- 1 teaspoon lemon juice
- Black pepper to the taste
- ½ cup avocado mayo
- ½ teaspoon sweet paprika
- 3 tablespoons olive oil
- 1 fennel bulb, chopped
- 1 yellow onion, chopped
- 2 garlic cloves, minced
- 1 cup canned tomatoes, no-salt-added and chopped
- 1 and ½ pounds big shrimp, peeled and deveined
- ¼ teaspoon saffron powder

Directions:

1. In a bowl, combine the garlic with lemon juice, black pepper, mayo and paprika and whisk.
2. Add the shrimp and toss.
3. Heat up a pan with the oil over medium-high heat, add the shrimp, fennel, onion and garlic mix, toss and cook for 4 minutes.
4. Add tomatoes and saffron, toss, divide into bowls and serve.

Enjoy!

Nutrition: calories 210, fat 2, fiber 5, carbs 8, protein 4

Cold Crab And Watermelon Soup

Preparation time: 4 hours

Cooking time: 0 minutes

Servings: 4

Ingredients:

- ¼ cup basil, chopped
- 2 pounds tomatoes
- 5 cups watermelon, cubed
- ¼ cup red wine vinegar
- 1/3 cup olive oil
- 2 garlic cloves, minced
- 1 zucchini, chopped
- Black pepper to the taste
- 1 cup crabmeat

Directions:

1. In your food processor, mix tomatoes with basil, vinegar, 4 cups watermelon, garlic, 1/3

cup oil and black pepper to the taste, pulse, pour into a bowl and keep in the fridge for 1 hour.

2. Divide this into bowls, add zucchini, crab and the rest of the watermelon and serve.

Enjoy!

Nutrition: calories 231, fat 3, fiber 3, carbs 6, protein 8

Shrimp And Orzo

Preparation time: 10 minutes

Cooking time: 30 minutes

Servings: 4

Ingredients:

- 1 pound shrimp, peeled and deveined
- Black pepper to the taste
- 3 garlic cloves, minced
- 1 tablespoon olive oil
- ½ teaspoon oregano, dried
- 1 yellow onion, chopped
- 2 cups low-sodium chicken stock
- 2 ounces orzo
- ½ cup water
- 4 ounces canned tomatoes, no-salt-added and chopped
- Juice of 1 lemon

Directions:

1. Heat up a pan with the oil over medium-high heat, add onion, garlic and oregano, stir and cook for 4 minutes.
2. Add orzo, stir and cook for 2 more minutes.
3. Add stock and the water, bring to a boil, cover, reduce heat to low and cook for 12 minutes.
4. Add lemon juice, tomatoes, black pepper and shrimp, introduce in the oven and bake at 400 degrees F for 15 minutes.
5. Divide between plates and serve.

Enjoy!

Nutrition: calories 228, fat 4, fiber 3, carbs 7, protein 8

Spanish Mussels Mix

Preparation time: 10 minutes

Cooking time: 23 minutes

Servings: 4

Ingredients:

- 3 tablespoons olive oil
- 2 pounds mussels, scrubbed
- Black pepper to the taste
- 3 cups canned tomatoes, crushed
- 1 shallot, chopped
- 2 garlic cloves, minced
- 2 cups low-sodium veggie stock
- 1/3 cup cilantro, chopped

Directions:

1. Heat up a pan with the oil over medium-high heat, add shallot, stir and cook for 3 minutes.

2. Add garlic, stock, tomatoes and black pepper, stir, bring to a simmer and cook for 10 minutes.
3. Add mussels and cilantro, toss, cover the pan, cook for another 10 minutes, divide into bowls and serve.

Enjoy!

Nutrition: calories 210, fat 2, fiber 6, carbs 5, protein 8

Scallops And Quinoa Salad

Preparation time: 10 minutes

Cooking time: 20 minutes

Servings: 6

Ingredients:

- 12 ounces sea scallops
- 4 tablespoons olive oil+ 2 teaspoons
- 4 teaspoons coconut aminos
- 1 and ½ cup quinoa, already cooked
- 2 teaspoons garlic, minced
- 1 cup snow peas, sliced
- 1/3 cup balsamic vinegar
- 1 cup scallions, sliced
- 1/3 cup red bell pepper, chopped
- ¼ cup cilantro, chopped

Directions:

1. In a bowl, mix scallops with half of the aminos and toss.

2. Heat up a pan with 1 tablespoon olive oil over medium heat, add quinoa, stir and cook for 8 minutes.
3. Add garlic and snow peas, stir, cook for 5 more minutes and take off heat.
4. Meanwhile, in a bowl, mix 3 tablespoons olive oil with the rest of the coconut aminos and vinegar, whisk well, add the quinoa mix, scallions and bell pepper and toss.
5. Heat up another pan with 2 teaspoons olive oil over medium-high heat, add scallops, cook for 1 minute on each side, add over the quinoa mix, toss a bit, sprinkle cilantro on top and serve.

Enjoy!

Nutrition: calories 221, fat 5, fiber 2, carbs 7, protein 8

Salmon And Veggies Soup

Preparation time: 10 minutes

Cooking time: 22 minutes

Servings: 6

Ingredients:

- 2 tablespoon olive oil
- 1 leek, chopped
- 1 red onion, chopped
- Black pepper to the taste
- 2 carrots, chopped
- 4 cups low-stock veggie stock
- 4 ounces salmon, skinless, boneless and cubed
- ½ cup coconut cream
- 1 tablespoon dill, chopped

Directions:

1. Heat up a pan with the oil over medium heat, add leek and onion, stir and cook for 7 minutes.
2. Add black pepper, add carrots and stock, stir, bring to a boil and cook for 10 minutes.
3. Add salmon, cream and dill, stir, boil everything for 5-6 minutes more, ladle into bowls and serve.

Enjoy!

Nutrition: calories 232, fat 3, fiber 4, carbs 7, protein 12

Salmon Salsa

Preparation time: 10 minutes

Cooking time: 0 minutes

Servings: 12

Ingredients:

- 3 yellow tomatoes, seedless and chopped
- 1 pound smoked salmon, boneless, skinless and flaked
- 1 red tomato, seedless and chopped
- Black pepper to the taste
- 1 cup watermelon, seedless and chopped
- 1 red onion, chopped
- 1 mango, peeled, seedless and chopped
- 2 jalapeno peppers, chopped
- ¼ cup parsley, chopped
- 3 tablespoons lime juice

Directions:

1. In a bowl, mix all the tomatoes with mango, watermelon, onion, salmon, black pepper, jalapeno, parsley and lime juice, toss and serve cold.

Enjoy!

Nutrition: calories 123, fat 2, fiber 4, carbs 5, protein 5

Salmon And Cucumber Salad

Preparation time: 10 minutes

Cooking time: 0 minutes

Servings: 4

Ingredients:

- 2 cucumbers, cubed
- 2 teaspoons lemon juice
- 4 ounces non-fat yogurt
- 1 teaspoon lemon zest, grated
- Black pepper to the taste
- 2 teaspoons dill, chopped
- 8 ounces smoked salmon, flaked

Directions:

1. In a bowl, the cucumbers with the lemon juice, lemon zest, black pepper, dill, salmon and yogurt, toss and serve cold.

Enjoy!

Nutrition: calories 242, fat 3, fiber 4, carbs 8, protein 3

Tuna Pate

Preparation time: 10 minutes

Cooking time: 0 minutes

Servings: 10

Ingredients:

- 6 ounces canned tuna, drained and flaked
- 3 teaspoons lemon juice
- 1 teaspoon onion, minced
- 8 ounces low-fat cream cheese
- ¼ cup parsley, chopped

Directions:

1. In a bowl, mix tuna with cream cheese, lemon juice, parsley and onion, stir really well and serve cold.

Enjoy!

Nutrition: calories 172, fat 2, fiber 3, carbs 8, protein 4

Shrimp And Avocado Salad

Preparation time: 10 minutes
Cooking time: 0 minutes
Servings: 2

Ingredients:

- 2 green onions, chopped
- 2 avocados, pitted, peeled and cut into medium chunks
- 2 tablespoons cilantro, chopped
- 1 cup shrimp, already cooked, peeled and deveined
- A pinch of salt and black pepper

Directions:

1. In a salad bowl, mix shrimp with avocado, green onions, cilantro, salt and pepper, toss and serve cold.

Enjoy!

Nutrition: calories 160, fat 2, fiber 3, carbs 10, protein 6

Shrimp And Cilantro Sauce

Preparation time: 10 minutes

Cooking time: 4 minutes

Servings: 2

Ingredients:

- 1 pound shrimp, peeled and deveined
- 3 tablespoons cilantro, chopped
- 3 tablespoons olive oil
- 1 tablespoon pine nuts
- Zest of 1 lemon, grated
- Juice of ½ lemon

Directions:

1. In your blender, combine the cilantro with 2 tablespoons oil, pine nuts, lemon zest and lemon juice and pulse well.
2. Heat up a pan with the rest of the oil over medium-high heat, add the shrimp and cook for 3 minutes.
3. Add the cilantro mix, toss, cook for 1 more minute, divide between plates and serve with a side salad.

Enjoy!

Nutrition: calories 210, fat 5, fiber 1, carbs 8, protein 12

Citrus Calamari

Preparation time: 10 minutes

Cooking time: 5 minutes

Servings: 4

Ingredients:

- 1 lime, sliced
- 1 lemon, sliced
- 2 pounds calamari tubes and tentacles, sliced
- Black pepper to the taste
- ¼ cup olive oil
- 2 garlic cloves, minced
- 3 tablespoons lemon juice
- 1 orange, peeled and cut into segments
- 2 tablespoons cilantro, chopped

Directions:

1. In a bowl, mix calamari with black pepper, lime slices, lemon slices, orange slices, garlic, oil, cilantro and lemon juice and toss.

2. Heat up a pan over medium-high heat, add calamari mix, cook for 5 minutes, divide into bowls and serve.

Enjoy!

Nutrition: calories 190, fat 2, fiber 1, carbs 11, protein 14

Mussels Curry

Preparation time: 10 minutes

Cooking time: 10 minutes

Servings: 4

Ingredients:

- 2 and ½ pounds mussels, scrubbed
- 14 ounces canned coconut milk
- 3 tablespoons red curry paste
- 1 tablespoon olive oil
- Black pepper to the taste
- ½ cup low-sodium chicken stock
- Juice of 1 lime
- Zest of 1 lime, grated
- ¼ cup cilantro, chopped
- 3 tablespoons basil, chopped

Directions:

1. Heat up a pan with the oil over medium-high heat, add curry paste, stir and cook for 2 minutes.
2. Add stock, black pepper, coconut milk, lime juice, lime zest and mussels, toss, cover the pan and cook for 10 minutes.
3. Divide this into bowls, sprinkle cilantro and basil on top and serve.

Enjoy!

Nutrition: calories 260, fat 12, fiber 2, carbs 10, protein 12

Salmon Casserole

Preparation time: 10 minutes

Cooking time: 1 hour

Servings: 4

Ingredients:

- 8 sweet potatoes, sliced
- 4 cups salmon, cooked and flaked
- 1 red onion, chopped
- 2 carrots, chopped
- Black pepper to the taste
- 1 celery stalk, chopped
- 2 cups coconut milk
- 3 tablespoons olive oil
- 2 tablespoons chives, chopped
- 2 garlic cloves, minced

Directions:

1. Heat up a pan with the oil over medium heat, add garlic, stir and cook for 1 minute.
2. Add coconut milk, black pepper, carrots, celery, chives, onion and salmon, stir and take off heat.
3. Arrange a layer of potatoes in a baking dish, add the salmon mix, top with the rest of the potatoes, introduce in the oven and bake at 375 degrees F for 1 hour.
4. Slice, divide between plates and serve.

Enjoy!

Nutrition: calories 220, fat 9, fiber 6, carbs 8, protein 12

Scallops And Cauliflower Mix

Preparation time: 10 minutes

Cooking time: 10 minutes

Servings: 4

Ingredients:

- 12 sea scallops
- 3 garlic cloves, minced
- Black pepper to the taste
- 2 cups cauliflower florets, chopped
- 2 tablespoons olive oil
- 2 cups sweet potatoes, chopped
- 1 tablespoon thyme, chopped
- ¼ cup pine nuts, toasted
- 1 cup low-sodium veggie stock
- 2 tablespoons chives, finely chopped

Directions:

1. Heat up a pan with the oil over medium-high heat, add thyme and garlic, stir and cook for 2 minutes.
2. Add scallops, cook them for 2 minutes, season them black pepper, add cauliflower, sweet potatoes and the stock, toss and cook for 5 minutes more.
3. Divide the scallops mix between plates, sprinkle chives and pine nuts on top and serve.

Enjoy!

Nutrition: calories 200, fat 10, fiber 4, carbs 9, protein 10

Spiced Salmon

Preparation time: 10 minutes

Cooking time: 10 minutes

Servings: 4

Ingredients:

- 4 salmon fillets
- 2 tablespoons olive oil
- 1 teaspoon cumin, ground
- 1 teaspoon sweet paprika
- 1 teaspoon onion powder
- 1 teaspoon chili powder
- ½ teaspoon garlic powder
- A pinch of salt and black pepper

Directions:

1. In a bowl, combine the cumin with paprika, onion powder, chili powder, garlic powder, salt and black pepper, toss and rub the salmon with this mix.

2. Heat up a pan with the oil over medium-high heat, add the salmon, cook for 5 minutes on each side, divide between plates and serve with a side salad.

Enjoy!

Nutrition: calories 220, fat 10, carbs 8, fiber 12, protein 10

Smoked Salmon And Tomatoes Salad

Preparation time: 10 minutes

Cooking time: 0 minutes

Servings: 2

Ingredients:

- 4 cups cherry tomatoes, halved
- 1 red onion, sliced
- 8 ounces smoked salmon, thinly sliced
- 4 tablespoons olive oil
- ½ teaspoon garlic, minced
- 2 tablespoons lemon juice
- 1 tablespoon oregano, chopped
- Black pepper to the taste
- 1 teaspoon balsamic vinegar

Directions:

1. In a salad bowl, combine the tomatoes with the onion, salmon, oil, garlic, lemon juice, oregano, black pepper and vinegar, toss and serve cold.

Enjoy!

Nutrition: calories 159, fat 8, fiber 3, carbs 7, protein 7

Coconut Cream Shrimp

Preparation time: 10 minutes
Cooking time: 0 minutes
Servings: 2

Ingredients:

- 1 pound shrimp, cooked, peeled and deveined
- 1 tablespoon coconut cream
- ¼ teaspoon jalapeno, chopped
- ½ teaspoon lime juice
- 1 tablespoon parsley, chopped
- A pinch of black pepper

Directions:

1. In a bowl, mix the shrimp with the cream, jalapeno, lime juice, parsley and black pepper, toss, divide into small bowls and serve.

Enjoy!

Nutrition: calories 183, fat 5, fiber 3, carbs 12, protein 8

Salmon And Mushroom Mix

Preparation time: 30 minutes

Cooking time: 10 minutes

Servings: 4

Ingredients:

- 8 ounces salmon fillets, boneless
- 2 tablespoons olive oil
- Black pepper to the taste
- 2 ounces white mushrooms, sliced
- ½ shallot, chopped
- 2 tablespoons balsamic vinegar
- 2 teaspoons mustard
- 3 tablespoons parsley, chopped

Directions:

1. Brush salmon fillets with 1 tablespoon olive oil, season with black pepper, place on preheated grill over medium heat, cook for 4 minutes on each side and divide between plates.
2. Heat up a pan with the rest of the oil over medium-high heat, add mushrooms, shallot and some black pepper, stir and cook for 5 minutes.
3. Add the mustard, the vinegar and the parsley, stir, cook for 2-3 minutes more, add over the salmon and serve.

Enjoy!

Nutrition: calories 220, fat 4, fiber 8, carbs 6, protein 12

Cod Sweet Potato Chowder

Preparation time: 10 minutes

Cooking time: 20 minutes

Servings: 4

Ingredients:

- 3 cups sweet potatoes, cubed
- 4 cod fillets, skinless and boneless
- 1 cup celery, chopped
- 1 cup onion, chopped
- Black pepper to the taste
- 2 tablespoons garlic, minced
- 2 tablespoons olive oil
- 2 tablespoons tomato paste, no-salt-added
- 3 cups veggie stock
- 1 and ½ cups tomatoes, chopped
- 1 and ½ teaspoons thyme

Directions:

1. Heat up a pot with the oil over medium heat, add tomato paste, celery, onion and garlic, stir and cook for 5 minutes.
2. Add tomatoes, tomato paste, potatoes and pepper, stir, bring to a boil, reduce heat and cook for 10 minutes.
3. Add thyme and cod, stir, cook for 5 minutes more, ladle into bowls and serve.

Enjoy!

Nutrition: calories 250, fat 6, fiber 5, carbs 7, protein 12

Simple Cinnamon Salmon

Preparation time: 10 minutes

Cooking time: 10 minutes

Servings: 2

Ingredients:

- 2 salmon fillets, boneless and skin-on
- Black pepper to the taste
- 1 tablespoon cinnamon powder
- 1 tablespoon olive oil

Directions:

1. Heat up a pan with the oil over medium heat, add pepper and cinnamon and stir well.
2. Add salmon, skin side up, cook for 5 minutes on each side, divide between plates and serve with a side salad.

Enjoy!

Nutrition: calories 220, fat 8, fiber 4, carbs 11, protein 8

Scallops And Strawberry Mix

Preparation time: 10 minutes

Cooking time: 6 minutes

Servings: 2

Ingredients:

- 4 ounces scallops
- ½ cup Pico de gallo
- ½ cup strawberries, chopped
- 1 tablespoon lime juice
- Black pepper to the taste

Directions:

1. Heat up a pan over medium heat, add scallops, cook for 3 minutes on each side and take off heat,
2. In a bowl, mix strawberries with lime juice, Pico de gallo, scallops and pepper, toss and serve cold.

Enjoy!

Nutrition: calories 169, fat 2, fiber 2, carbs 8, protein 13

Baked Haddock

Preparation time: 10 minutes

Cooking time: 30 minutes

Servings: 4

Ingredients:

- 1 pound haddock, boneless
- 3 teaspoons water
- 2 tablespoons lemon juice
- A pinch of salt and black pepper
- 2 tablespoons avocado mayonnaise
- 1 teaspoon dill, chopped
- Cooking spray

Directions:

1. Spray a baking dish with some cooking oil, add fish, water, lemon juice, salt, black pepper, mayo and dill, toss, introduce in the oven and bake at 350 degrees F for 30 minutes.
2. Divide between plates and serve.

Enjoy!

Nutrition: calories 264, fat 4, fiber 5, carbs 7, protein 12

Basil Tilapia

Preparation time: 10 minutes

Cooking time: 10 minutes

Servings: 4

Ingredients:

- 4 tilapia fillets, boneless
- Black pepper to the taste
- ½ cup low-fat parmesan, grated
- 4 tablespoons avocado mayonnaise
- 2 teaspoons basil, dried
- 2 tablespoons lemon juice
- ¼ cup olive oil

Directions:

1. Grease a baking dish with the oil, add tilapia fillets, black pepper, spread mayo, basil, drizzle lemon juice and top with the parmesan, introduce in preheated broiler and cook over medium-high heat for 5 minutes on each side.
2. Divide between plates and serve with a side salad.

Enjoy!

Nutrition: calories 215, fat 10, fiber 5, carbs 7, protein 11

Salmon Meatballs

Preparation time: 10 minutes

Cooking time: 30 minutes

Servings: 4

Ingredients:

- Cooking spray
- 2 garlic cloves, minced
- 1 yellow onion, chopped
- 1 pound wild salmon, boneless and minced
- ¼ cup chives, chopped
- 1 egg
- 2 tablespoons Dijon mustard
- 1 tablespoon coconut flour
- A pinch of salt and black pepper

Directions:

1. In a bowl, mix onion with garlic, salmon, chives, coconut flour, salt, pepper, mustard and egg, stir well, shape medium meatballs,

arrange them on a baking sheet, grease them with cooking spray, introduce in the oven at 350 degrees F and bake for 25 minutes.

2. Divide the meatballs between plates and serve with a side salad.

Enjoy!

Nutrition: calories 211, fat 4, fiber 1, carbs 6, protein 13

Tuna Cakes

Preparation time: 10 minutes

Cooking time: 10 minutes

Servings: 12

Ingredients:

- 15 ounces canned tuna, drain well and flaked
- 3 eggs
- ½ teaspoon dill, dried
- 1 teaspoon parsley, dried
- ½ cup red onion, chopped
- 1 teaspoon garlic powder
- A pinch of salt and black pepper
- Olive oil for frying

Directions:

1. In a bowl, mix tuna with salt, pepper, dill, parsley, onion, garlic powder and eggs, stir and shape medium cakes out of this mix.
2. Heat up a pan with oil over medium-high heat, add tuna cakes, cook for 5 minutes on each side, divide between plates and serve with a side salad.

Enjoy!

Nutrition: calories 210, fat 2, fiber 2, carbs 6, protein 6

Italian Shrimp

Preparation time: 10 minutes

Cooking time: 22 minutes

Servings: 4

Ingredients:

- 8 ounces mushrooms, chopped
- 1 asparagus bunch, cut into medium pieces
- 1 pound shrimp, peeled and deveined
- Black pepper to the taste
- 2 tablespoons olive oil
- 2 teaspoons Italian seasoning
- 1 yellow onion, chopped
- 1 teaspoon red pepper flakes, crushed
- 1 cup low-fat parmesan cheese, grated
- 2 garlic cloves, minced
- 1 cup coconut cream

Directions:

1. Put water in a pot, bring to a boil over medium heat, add asparagus, steam for 2 minutes, transfer to a bowl with ice water, drain and put in a bowl.
2. Heat up a pan with the oil over medium heat, add onions and mushrooms, stir and cook for 7 minutes.
3. Add pepper flakes, Italian seasoning, black pepper and asparagus, stir and cook for 5 minutes more.
4. Add cream, shrimp, garlic and parmesan, toss, cook for 7 minutes, divide into bowls and serve.

Enjoy!

Nutrition: calories 225, fat 6, fiber 5, carbs 6, protein 8

Shrimp, Bamboo And Snow Peas Soup

Preparation time: 10 minutes

Cooking time: 10 minutes

Servings: 4

Ingredients:

- 4 scallions, chopped
- 1 and ½ tablespoons olive oil
- 1 teaspoon garlic, minced
- 8 cups low-sodium chicken stock
- ¼ cup coconut aminos
- 5 ounces canned bamboo shots, no-salt-added sliced
- Black pepper to the taste
- 1 pound shrimp, peeled and deveined
- ½ pound snow peas

Directions:

1. Heat up a pot with the oil over medium heat, add scallions and ginger, stir and cook for 2 minutes.
2. Add coconut aminos, stock and black pepper, stir and bring to a boil.
3. Add shrimp, snow peas and bamboo shots, stir, cook for 5 minutes, ladle into bowls and serve.

Enjoy!

Nutrition: calories 200, fat 3, fiber 2, carbs 4, protein 14

Lemony Mussels

Preparation time: 5 minutes

Cooking time: 5 minutes

Servings: 4

Ingredients:

- 2 pound mussels, scrubbed
- 2 garlic cloves, minced
- 1 tablespoon olive oil
- Juice of 1 lemon

Directions:

1. Put some water in a pot, add mussels, bring to a boil over medium heat, cook for 5 minutes, discard unopened mussels and transfer them to a bowl.
2. In another bowl, mix the oil with garlic and lemon juice, whisk well, add over the mussels, toss and serve.

Enjoy!

Nutrition: calories 140, fat 4, fiber 4, carbs 8, protein 8

Salmon And Quinoa Salad

Preparation time: 10 minutes

Cooking time: 10 minutes

Servings: 1

Ingredients:

- 1 medium salmon fillet, boneless
- 1 teaspoon olive oil
- A pinch of black pepper
- Cooking spray
- 1 and ½ cups kale, chopped
- ½ cup quinoa, already cooked
- 1 tablespoon lemon juice
- 5 red grapes, halved

Directions:

1. Put the salmon in a baking dish greased with cooking spray, drizzle the oil over the fish, season with black pepper and bake in the oven at 425 degrees F for 10 minutes.

2. Meanwhile, in a bowl, combine the quinoa with the grapes, kale and lemon juice and toss well.
3. Arrange the salmon on a plate, add the quinoa salad next to it and serve.

Enjoy!

Nutrition: calories 261, fat 5, fiber 7, carbs 10, protein 15

Salmon And Horseradish Sauce

Preparation time: 10 minutes

Cooking time: 10 minutes

Servings: 4

Ingredients:

- 1 and ½ tablespoons olive oil
- 4 medium salmon fillets, boneless and skin-on
- ½ cup coconut cream
- A pinch of black pepper
- 2 tablespoons dill, chopped
- 1 tablespoon prepared horseradish

Directions:

1. Heat up a pan with the oil over medium-high heat, add salmon fillets, season with black pepper and cook for 5 minutes one each side.
2. In a bowl, combine the cream with the dill and horseradish and whisk well.
3. Divide the salmon between plates and serve with the horseradish cream on top.

Enjoy!

Nutrition: calories 275, fat 12, fiber 4, carbs 14, protein 27

Tuna Salad

Preparation time: 10 minutes

Cooking time: 0 minutes

Servings: 2

Ingredients:

- 2 teaspoons olive oil
- 1 teaspoon red vinegar
- ½ teaspoon lemon juice
- ½ teaspoon mustard
- A pinch of black pepper
- ½ cup already cooked quinoa
- ¼ cup canned chickpeas, no-salt-added, drained and rinsed
- ¼ cup cucumber, chopped
- 5 cherry tomatoes, halved
- 5 ounces white tuna canned in water, drained
- 1 tablespoon low-fat cheese, crumbled

Directions:

1. In a salad bowl, combine the quinoa with chickpeas, cucumber, tomatoes, tuna and cheese and toss.
2. Add black pepper, oil, vinegar, lemon juice and mustard, toss well and serve.

Enjoy!

Nutrition: calories 241, fat 4, fiber 5, carbs 12, protein 14

Cod And Tasty Relish

Preparation time: 10 minutes

Cooking time: 10 minutes

Servings: 4

Ingredients:

- 1 and ½ tablespoons oregano, chopped
- 1 cup peas
- 2 tablespoons shallots, chopped
- 2 tablespoons lime juice
- 2 tablespoons capers
- 3 tablespoons olive oil
- A pinch of black pepper
- 4 medium cod fillets, boneless

Directions:

1. Heat up a pan with 1 tablespoon oil over medium-high heat, add the cod fillets, cook for 5 minutes on each side and divide between plates.
2. In a bowl, combine the oregano with the peas, shallots, lime juice, capers, black pepper and 2 tablespoons oil and toss well.
3. Divide this next to the cod and serve.

Enjoy!

Nutrition: calories 221, fat 11, fiber 3, carbs 8, protein 20

Smoked Salmon Mix

Preparation time: 10 minutes

Cooking time: 0 minutes

Servings: 4

Ingredients:

- 2 tablespoons dill, chopped
- 1 teaspoons lemon zest, grated
- 8 ounces low-fat cream cheese
- A pinch of black pepper
- 1 pound smoked salmon, flaked
- 7 ounces cucumber, sliced
- ¼ cup shallot, chopped
- 2 tablespoons mint, chopped

Directions:

1. In a bowl, combine the dill with lemon zest, cream cheese, black pepper, salmon, cucumber, shallot and mint and toss well.
2. Serve cold with whole wheat bread slices.

Enjoy!

Nutrition: calories 277, fat 4, fiber 6, carbs 15, protein 15

Halibut And Kale Pesto

Preparation time: 10 minutes

Cooking time: 6 minutes

Servings: 4

Ingredients:

- 2 tablespoons almonds, chopped
- 2 garlic cloves
- 4 cups kale, torn
- ½ cup olive oil+1 tablespoon
- ¼ cup low-fat parmesan, grated
- 2 tablespoons lemon juice
- A pinch of black pepper
- 4 halibut fillets
- 1 pound cherry tomatoes, halved

Directions:

1. In a blender, combine the almonds with the garlic, kale, ½ cup oil, lemon juice and parmesan and pulse well.
2. Heat up a pan with 1 tablespoon oil over medium-high heat, add the fish, season with black pepper, cook for 3 minutes on each side and divide between plates
3. Serve with the cherry tomatoes on the side and with the kale pesto on top.

Enjoy!

Nutrition: calories 261, fat 4, fiber 7, carbs 14, protein 14

Simple Grilled Tilapia

Preparation time: 10 minutes

Cooking time: 8 minutes

Servings: 4

Ingredients:

- 1 and ½ tablespoons olive oil
- 1 teaspoon smoked paprika
- ½ teaspoon garlic powder
- A pinch of black pepper
- 4 medium tilapia fillets

Directions:

1. Heat up a pan with the oil over medium-high heat, season the fish with paprika, garlic powder and black pepper, add it to the pan, cook for 4 minutes on each side, divide between plates and serve with a side salad.

Enjoy!

Nutrition: calories 222, fat 4, fiber 4, carbs 14, protein 25

Delicious Arctic Char

Preparation time: 10 minutes
Cooking time: 8 minutes
Servings: 4

Ingredients:

- 1 cup orange segments
- 1 tablespoon parsley, chopped
- 2 tablespoons red onions, chopped
- 1 tablespoon capers, chopped
- 1 teaspoon orange zest, grated
- 1 tablespoon orange juice
- 1 tablespoon olive oil
- 1 teaspoon balsamic vinegar
- A pinch of black pepper
- Cooking spray
- 4 arctic char fillets

Directions:

1. Grease a pan with cooking spray, add fish fillets, season with black pepper, cook for 4 minutes on each side and divide between plates.
2. In a bowl, combine the orange with parsley, onions, capers, orange zest, orange juice, oil and vinegar and toss well.
3. Divide this on top of the fish fillets and serve.

Enjoy!

Nutrition: calories 231, fat 12, fiber 3, carbs 8, protein 14

Tasty Halibut And Cherry Tomatoes

Preparation time: 10 minutes

Cooking time: 13 minutes

Servings: 4

Ingredients:

- 1 and ½ tablespoon olive oil
- 4 halibut fillets, skinless
- 2 cups cherry tomatoes
- A pinch of black pepper
- 3 garlic cloves, minced
- 2 tablespoons balsamic vinegar
- 2 tablespoons basil, chopped

Directions:

1. Heat up a pan with 1 tablespoon olive oil, add halibut fillets, cook them for 5 minutes on each side and divide between plates.

2. Heat up another pan with the rest of the oil over medium-high heat, add the tomatoes, garlic, vinegar and basil, toss, cook for 3 minutes, add next to the fish and serve.

Enjoy!

Nutrition: calories 221, fat 4 fiber 1, carbs 6, protein 21

Salmon And Sauce

Preparation time: 10 minutes
Cooking time: 10 minutes
Servings: 4

Ingredients:

- 1 and ½ tablespoons avocado mayonnaise
- 3 tablespoons non-fat yogurt
- 1 and ½ tablespoons mustard
- 2 tablespoons dill, chopped
- 2 tablespoons lemon juice
- A pinch of black pepper
- 1 garlic clove minced
- 4 salmon fillets, boneless
- Cooking spray

Directions:

1. Grease a baking dish with cooking spray, arrange the salmon fillets in the dish and season them with black pepper.
2. In a bowl, combine the mayo with the yogurt, mustard, dill, lemon juice, black pepper, whisk, pour over the fish, introduce in the oven and cook at 425 degrees F for 10 minutes.
3. Divide everything between plates and serve.

Enjoy!

Nutrition: calories 261, fat 12, fiber 3, carbs 8, protein 16

Arctic Char And Cucumber Relish

Preparation time: 10 minutes

Cooking time: 6 minutes

Servings: 2

Ingredients:

- ¾ cup cucumber, chopped
- ¼ cup shallots, chopped
- 1 tablespoon cilantro, chopped
- 2 teaspoons mint, chopped
- 2 teaspoons lemon juice
- ½ teaspoon mustard
- A pinch of black pepper
- 1 tablespoon olive oil
- 2 arctic char fillets

Directions:

1. Season the fish with black pepper, drizzle the oil, arrange them in a baking dish, introduce in the oven and bake at 425 degrees F for 6 minutes.

2. In a bowl, combine the cucumber with the shallots, cilantro, mint, lemon juice and mustard, toss well, add next to the fish and serve.

Enjoy!

Nutrition: calories 231, fat 3, fiber 6, carbs 9, protein 22

Soft Parsley Salmon

Preparation time: 10 minutes

Cooking time: 15 minutes

Servings: 6

Ingredients:

- 3 tablespoons olive oil
- 3 tablespoons mustard
- 5 teaspoons stevia
- ½ cup whole wheat breadcrumbs
- ½ cup pecans, chopped
- 6 salmon fillets, boneless
- 2 tablespoons parsley, chopped
- Black pepper to the taste

=

Directions:

1. In a bowl, mix mustard with oil and stevia and whisk.
2. In another bowl, mix pecans with parsley and breadcrumbs.

3. Season salmon fillets with black pepper to the taste, put in a baking dish brush with mustard mixture, top with breadcrumbs mix, introduce in the oven and bake at 400 degrees F for 15 minutes.
4. Divide between plates and serve with a side salad.

Enjoy!

Nutrition: calories 230, fat 4, fiber 2, carbs 14, protein 12

Salmon And Cauliflower Mix

Preparation time: 10 minutes

Cooking time: 20 minutes

Servings: 4

Ingredients:

- ¼ cup coconut sugar
- 2 tablespoons coconut aminos
- 1 cauliflower head, florets separated
- 4 salmon fillets, boneless
- 1 big red onion, cut into wedges
- 2 tablespoons olive oil
- Black pepper to the taste

Directions:

1. In a small bowl, mix sugar with coconut aminos and whisk.
2. Heat up a pan with half of the oil over medium-high heat, add cauliflower and onion, stir and cook for 10 minutes.
3. Put the salmon in a baking dish, drizzle the rest of the oil, add coconut aminos, toss a bit, season with black pepper, introduce in the oven and bake at 400 degrees F for 10 minutes.
4. Divide the salmon and the cauliflower mix between plates and serve.

Enjoy!

Nutrition: calories 220, fat 3, fiber 3, carbs 12, protein 9

Salmon And Peaches Mix

Preparation time: 10 minutes
Cooking time: 10 minutes
Servings: 4

Ingredients:

- 1 tablespoon balsamic vinegar
- 1 teaspoon thyme, chopped
- 1 tablespoon ginger, grated
- 4 tablespoons olive oil
- Black pepper to the taste
- 2 red onions, cut into wedges
- 3 peaches cut into wedges
- 4 salmon steaks

Directions:

1. In a small bowl, combine vinegar with ginger, thyme, 3 tablespoons olive oil and black pepper and whisk

2. In another bowl, mix onion with peaches, 1 tablespoon oil and pepper and toss.

3. Season salmon with black pepper, place on preheated grill over medium heat, cook for 5 minutes on each side and divide between plates.

4. Put the peaches and onions on the same grill, cook for 4 minutes on each side, divide next to the salmon, drizzle the vinegar mix and serve.

Enjoy!

Nutrition: calories 200, fat 2, fiber 2, carbs 3, protein 2

Salmon And Beans Mix

Preparation time: 10 minutes

Cooking time: 20 minutes

Servings: 4

Ingredients:

- 2 tablespoons coconut aminos
- ½ cup olive oil
- 1 and ½ cup low-sodium chicken stock
- 6 ounces salmon fillets
- 2 garlic cloves, minced
- 1 tablespoon ginger, grated
- 1 cup canned black beans, no-salt-added, drained and rinsed
- 2 teaspoons balsamic vinegar
- ¼ cup radishes, grated
- ¼ cup carrots, grated
- ¼ cup scallions, chopped

Directions:

1. In a bowl, combine the aminos with half of the oil and whisk.
2. Put the salmon in a baking dish, pour add coconut aminos and the stock, toss a bit, leave aside in the fridge for 10 minutes, introduce in preheated broiler and cook over medium-high heat for 4 minutes on each side.
3. Heat up a pan with the rest of the oil over medium heat, add garlic, ginger and black beans, stir and cook for 3 minutes.
4. Add vinegar, radishes, carrots and scallions, toss and cook for 5 minutes more.
5. Divide fish and the black beans mix between plates and serve.

Enjoy!

Nutrition: calories 220, fat 4, fiber 2, carbs 12, protein 7

Salmon And Pomegranate Mix

Preparation time: 20 minutes

Cooking time: 10 minutes

Servings: 4

Ingredients:

- 1 tablespoon olive oil
- 4 salmon fillets, skinless and boneless
- 4 tablespoons sesame paste
- Juice of 1 lemon
- 1 lemon, cut into wedges
- ½ cucumber, chopped
- Seeds from 1 pomegranate
- A bunch of parsley, chopped

Directions:

1. Heat up a pan with the oil over medium heat, add salmon, cook for 5 minutes on each side and divide between plates

2. In a bowl, mix sesame paste and lemon juice and whisk.
3. Add cucumber, parsley and pomegranate seeds and toss
4. Divide this over the salmon and serve..

Enjoy!

Nutrition: calories 254, fat 3, fiber 6, carbs 9, protein 14

Salmon And Veggie Mix

Preparation time: 10 minutes

Cooking time: 30 minutes

Servings: 6

Ingredients:

- 3 red onions, cut into wedges
- ¾ cup green olives, pitted
- 3 red bell peppers, cut into strips
- ½ teaspoon smoked paprika
- Black pepper to the taste
- 5 tablespoons olive oil
- 6 salmon fillets, skinless and boneless
- 2 tablespoons parsley, chopped

Directions:

1. Spread bell peppers, onions and olives on a lined baking sheet, add smoked paprika, black pepper and 3 tablespoons olive oil, toss to coat, bake in the oven at 375 degrees F for 15 minutes and divide between plates.

2. Heat up a pan with the rest of the oil over medium-high heat, add the salmon, season with black pepper, cook for 5 minutes on each side, divide next to the bell peppers and olives mix, sprinkle parsley on top and serve.

Enjoy!

Nutrition: calories 221, fat 2, fiber 3, carbs 8, protein 10

Greek Salmon

Preparation time: 10 minutes

Cooking time: 15 minutes

Servings: 4

Ingredients:

- 4 medium salmon fillets, skinless and boneless
- 1 fennel bulb, chopped
- Black pepper to the taste
- ¼ cup low-sodium veggie stock
- 1 cup non-fat yogurt
- ¼ cup green olives pitted and chopped
- ¼ cup chives, chopped
- 1 tablespoon olive oil
- 1 tablespoon lemon juice

Directions:

1. Arrange the fennel in a baking dish, add salmon fillets, season with black pepper, add

stock, bake in the oven at 390 degrees F for 10 minutes and divide everything between plates.

2. In a bowl, mix yogurt with chives, olives, lemon juice, olive oil and black pepper and whisk well.

3. Top the salmon with this mix and serve.

Enjoy!

Nutrition: calories 252, fat 2, fiber 4, carbs 12, protein 9

Creamy Salmon And Asparagus Mix

Preparation time: 10 minutes

Cooking time: 10 minutes

Servings: 6

Ingredients:

- 1 tablespoon lemon zest, grated
- 1 tablespoon lemon juice
- Black pepper to the taste
- 1 cup coconut cream
- 1 pound asparagus, trimmed
- 20 ounces salmon, skinless and boneless
- 1-ounce parmesan cheese, grated

Directions:

1. Put some water in a pot, add a pinch of salt, bring to a boil over medium heat, add asparagus, cook for 1 minute, transfer to a bowl filled with ice water, drain and put in a bowl.

2. Heat up the pot with the water again over medium heat, add salmon, cook for 5 minutes and also drain.
3. In a bowl, mix lemon peel with cream and lemon juice and whisk
4. Heat up a pan over medium-high heat, asparagus, cream and pepper, cook for 1 more minute, divide between plates, add salmon and serve with grated parmesan.

Enjoy!

Nutrition: calories 354, fat 2, fiber 2, carbs 2, protein 4

Easy Salmon And Brussels Sprouts

Preparation time: 10 minutes

Cooking time: 20 minutes

Servings: 6

Ingredients:

- 2 tablespoons brown sugar
- 1 teaspoon onion powder
- 1 teaspoon garlic powder
- 1 teaspoon smoked paprika
- 3 tablespoons olive oil
- 1 and ¼ pounds Brussels sprouts, halved
- 6 medium salmon fillets, boneless

Directions:

1. In a bowl, mix sugar with onion powder, garlic powder, smoked paprika and 2 tablespoon olive oil and whisk well.

2. Spread Brussels sprouts on a lined baking sheet, drizzle the rest of the olive oil, toss to coat, introduce in the oven at 450 degrees F and bake for 5 minutes.
3. Add salmon fillets brush with sugar mix you've prepared, introduce in the oven and bake for 15 minutes more.
4. Divide everything between plates and serve.

Enjoy!

Nutrition: calories 212, fat 5, fiber 3, carbs 12, protein 8

THANK YOU

Thank you for choosing *Fresh Summer Recipes with Fish and Seafood* for improving your cooking skills! I hope you enjoyed making the recipes as much as tasting them! If you're interested in learning new recipes and new meals to cook, go and check out the other books of the series.

CPSIA information can be obtained
at www.ICGtesting.com
Printed in the USA
BVHW041725090621
609091BV00016B/2663